FAMOUS LIVES

The Story of
WALT DISNEY
Maker of Magical Worlds

FAMOUS LIVES
titles in Large-Print Editions:

FAMOUS LIVES

The Story of
WALT DISNEY
Maker of Magical Worlds

By Bernice Selden

Gareth Stevens Publishing
MILWAUKEE

For my son, Josh Kornbluth — as talented
as Disney, as adorable as Mickey.

For a free color catalog describing Gareth Stevens' list of high-quality books and
multimedia programs, call 1-800-542-2595 (USA) or 1-800-461-9120 (Canada).
Gareth Stevens Publishing's Fax: (414) 225-0377.
See our catalog, too, on the World Wide Web: http://gsinc.com

Library of Congress Cataloging-in-Publication Data

Selden, Bernice.
    The story of Walt Disney : maker of magical worlds / by Bernice Selden.
        p. cm. – (Famous lives)
    Includes index.
    Summary: Describes the life of Walt Disney, from his childhood on a Missouri farm through his
years as a cartoonist and filmmaker to his creation of his Magic Kingdoms in California and Florida.
    ISBN 0-8368-1468-1 (lib. bdg.)
    1. Disney, Walt, 1901-1966–Juvenile literature. 2. Animators–United States–Biography–
Juvenile literature. [1. Disney, Walt, 1901-1966. 2. Motion pictures–Biography.] I. Title.
II. Series: Famous lives (Milwaukee, Wis.)
NC1766.U52D558 1996
791.43'092–dc20   95-53809
[B]

The events described in this book are true. They have been carefully researched and
excerpted from authentic biographies, writings, and commentaries. No part of this biography
has been fictionalized. To learn more about Walt Disney, refer to the list of books and videos
at the back of this book or ask your librarian to recommend other fine books and videos.

First published in this edition in North America in 1996 by
Gareth Stevens Publishing
1555 North RiverCenter Drive, Suite 201
Milwaukee, Wisconsin 53212 USA

Original © 1989 by Parachute Press, Inc. as a Yearling Biography.
Published by arrangement with Bantam Doubleday Dell Books for Young Readers,
a division of Bantam Doubleday Dell Publishing Group, Inc.
Additional end matter © 1996 by Gareth Stevens, Inc.

PICTURE CREDITS: Cover illustration: Chet Jezierski; AP/Wide World Photos: pp. 47,
48, 50 (bottom), 51 (bottom), 54; Alan D. Levenson/Time Magazine: p. 53 (bottom);
The Museum of Modern Art/Film Stills Archive: pp. 51 (top), 52, 53 (top); Mark
Wanamaker/Bison Archives: pp. 49, 50 (top). Special thanks to the Walt Disney Company.

Printed in the United States of America

1 2 3 4 5 6 7 8 9 99 98 97 96

Contents

Hog Rider

When Diane Disney was six years old she went to her father with a very important question. "Are you Walt Disney?" she asked.

"Of course, darling," her father said. "Who did you *think* I was?"

"What I mean is . . . are you the *famous* Walt Disney who makes movies? Someone at school said you were."

Her father grinned and nodded.

Diane blushed. Then she held out a piece of paper and said, "Can I have your autograph?"

Taking out his fountain pen, Walt dashed off his famous signature with a flourish.

"Oh, thank you, Daddy!" she gasped. It was as if he had handed her the world.

The year was 1939, and by then Walt Disney's name was known around the globe. Whenever anyone thought of cartoons, it was Disney who came to mind. He was the creator of the lovable cartoon characters Mickey Mouse and Donald Duck. He had been one of the first to successfully bring sound and color to movies. His *Snow White and the Seven Dwarfs,* a full-length animated film, had been a smash success wherever it was shown. Hollywood had honored him with many Oscar awards for his outstanding work in the movie industry. Later in his life, he would create two of the most famous amusement parks in the world, Disneyland and Walt Disney World.

How did it all begin?
Walt was born in the year 1901 in a small town just outside of Chicago. Elias Disney, Walt's father, was very active in his church. He not only gave the church what little money he could, he even climbed up on a ladder with hammer and nails and helped rebuild it. He was, at the time, a builder by trade.

The minister of the church, Walter Parr, discovered that Elias's wife, Flora, was expecting her fourth child at the same time that his own wife was expecting a child. This gave him an idea.

"If your wife has a son, you name him after me," the minister said. "And if my wife has one, we will christen him Elias, after you."

The boys were born within a day of each other and were named Elias Parr and Walter Elias Disney. There were already three boys in the family when Walt was born: Herbert, Raymond, and Roy. A girl, Ruth, was born two years later.

Walt's childhood was not an easy one. As an adult he brought so much happiness to so many children, but he was not always a happy boy. The Disney family moved often from one town to another, so Walt spent his childhood in many different places. "Pa always had ants in his pants," one of the sons said of Elias. "He could never stay any place long enough to warm a seat."

No sooner did the children get used to life in a busy city than they would be hauled off to the countryside. And then, a few years later, they would find themselves back in the city again.

It was the town of Marceline, in Missouri, that Walt remembered most fondly. In 1906 when Walt was five years old, Elias bought forty-eight acres of farmland and filled it with cows, pigs, chickens, ducks, and pigeons. There was a beautiful green lawn in back of the house with weeping willow trees, and there were two big apple orchards.

"We had every kind of apple you ever heard of," Walt remembered. "There was one kind called Wolf River. Wolf River apples were tremendous in size. People came from miles around to see ours."

Each of the Disney children shared responsibilities on the farm. When Elias built the pigpen, it was five-year-old Walt's job to keep his eye on the pigs. One pig, Porky, was especially fond of Walt. She came right up to the house and pressed her snout against the window to look for him.

Walt liked to sit on top of the pig, but she did not make it very easy for him to ride her. Walt would get on Porky's back, cling to her pointy ears, and together they would set out for a particularly muddy pool.

Porky would slosh into the water and plod halfway across. Then she would stand stock-still, give a shudder with her whole body, and settle straight down into the water. Smack into the murky mess Walt would go. Porky seemed to enjoy the joke, and Walt didn't seem to mind the mess!

Walt called the other farm animals by name also. There was a hen named Martha, who would come out of the henhouse when he called and lay an egg right in his hand. In the morning, when Walt walked to the barn, he would greet each animal he passed. These animals that Walt loved as a child were early inspirations for the unforgettable creatures that later came to life in his animated movies.

Another of his favorites was Rupert, a horse. Rupert belonged to Marceline's favorite doctor, old "Doc" Sherwood. The doctor was very friendly to Walt and often took him along in his buggy when he visited people who were sick.

Doc Sherwood knew that Walt had artistic talent. Once, Walt had taken a brush and some tar and drawn pictures of animals all over the white walls of the farmhouse. Walt was punished for drawing on the walls, but this incident gave Walt's aunt an idea. She gave Walt a pad of paper and a box of pencils to encourage his artistic talent—on paper!

One day, when Walt was about seven, Doc Sherwood invited him to bring his pencils and pad to his house. He wanted Walt to draw a portrait of Rupert the horse. He promised that if the picture was good, he would buy it for a nickel.

Rupert was restless that day, and Walt had to change positions many times to keep the horse's profile in view. Finally he finished. The doctor pronounced the drawing very good and paid Walt the nickel. Even as a small boy, Walt was able to earn money by using his talent!

Life on the farm was usually happy for Walt. But sometimes it was hard. One year there was a long spell without rain. The Disney farm was not doing well. When nobody came to buy the family's apples, Walt's mother started selling eggs and butter to people living nearby.

Times were so bad that Elias would not allow his own family to eat any of the butter that they churned. All of it was put aside to sell to others.

But Flora found a way to get around that rule. When her husband wasn't looking, she would spread the butter in a thick layer on slices of bread. Then she would pass a slice to each of her children, *with the buttered side down.* Walt and his brothers and sister took careful bites so Elias would not catch on.

Elias was a difficult man. No matter how much his sons did for him, it never seemed to be enough. In his eyes, there was almost nothing that they did right. He often gave the boys beatings. But as Herbert, Raymond, and Roy grew too old to be punished this way, only Walt was left to punish.

One day Roy said to Walt, "You know, kid, you don't have to take this kind of abuse, even from Father." Walt made up his mind that he would not take even one more whipping.

One day soon after, Elias asked Walt to hand him a tool. Walt ran to get it but was not quick enough to please his father. Elias scolded him. Walt answered back. This made Elias even more furious. Children were not supposed to argue with their parents. Elias told Walt to go down to the basement. When they got there, he took a strap down from its peg on the wall. But when Elias lifted the strap, he could not move. Walt had grabbed his wrist and would not let go.

"You cannot hit me, Father," Walt said quietly. "Not any more." His heart thumped in his chest. What would happen next?

Walt was stunned to see his father begin to cry. The face that moments before had been twisted in anger was suddenly wet with tears. From that point on, there were no more beatings.

But things did not get better on the farm.

After his crops failed for the second year, Elias was forced to borrow money from the bank by taking out a mortgage on the farm. The older boys, Herbert and Raymond, had been promised a bit of land for themselves. Now Elias told them it was not possible. When they protested, he scolded them in his usual harsh manner.

Herbert and Raymond had worked hard on the farm, but they had not been paid for their work in a long while. Now that they were refused a part of the land, they could find no reason to stay. The two young men ran away from home. They found jobs of their own, but they didn't forget their younger brothers and sister. Soon they sent their old clothes to Flora to be cut down for Roy and Walt.

One day, not long after the boys had left, Elias became ill with a high fever. It was discovered that the well water was contaminated, and Elias had gotten typhoid from the bad water. Typhoid often caused death. But Elias got better, although he remained very weak. Flora couldn't run the farm herself. There was nothing she could do but sell it. Elias had often talked of moving to Kansas City. They decided, now, that perhaps he could do better there.

That winter of 1909 was one of the coldest

the Midwest had ever seen. Flora wrapped the boys in blankets and gave them bricks she had heated on the stove to warm their feet. Together, Roy and Walt rode around Marceline in a little sleigh driven by a horse. They went everywhere posting notices saying that the farm property would be sold the following week. Once everything was sold and the boys finished the school term, the Disney family moved to Kansas City.

Comedy Act

Kansas City in 1910 was a lively and prosperous place. Here Elias hoped to earn a decent living at last.

He bought delivery rights to the famous newspaper, the *Kansas City Star*. His job was to provide doorstep delivery of morning and evening papers to a thousand people.

Elias was still too weak from typhoid to work himself, so he employed a team of boys, including Roy and Walt. But there was a big difference between Elias's sons and the other boys who earned three dollars a week. Roy and Walt did not receive any money at all. When they asked their father why they did not get paid, Elias said sternly, "I provide you with clothing and I feed you. That's enough."

17

Roy was seventeen and no longer in school. He could give all his time and energy to the business. But Walt was nine years old and still a schoolboy. He never forgot all the cold, dark mornings when his father shook him awake. At three-thirty in the morning, he struggled out of bed. Sometimes he nodded off while he tied his shoelaces. Then sleepy young Walt would go out to the street to meet the newspaper delivery trucks.

Most delivery boys rode on bicycles and threw the papers onto the porches. But Elias wanted to show that his service was better than all the others.

Elias's employees were not allowed to use bicycles at all. They had to carry the newspapers up to the porches and lay them down flat. If it was windy, they were supposed to put a brick on top of the newspaper. If it was raining or snowing, they had to put them behind the storm doors.

Walt never forgot how hard his life was in those days: how he climbed the icy porch steps with snow up to his knees, slipping and sliding, with tears running down his cheeks from the cold.

Some of the apartment houses had steam heat. Walt would curl up for a few minutes in the lobby of one of them, just to get warm. The next thing he knew, the sun was up—he had fallen fast asleep! Then he could not remember which apartments had gotten their papers and which had not. Up he would go, back to the top floor, to check every door.

When he was a grown man, Walt had the same nightmare over and over again. He dreamed that he had missed a customer on the route. Then he would wake up in a sweat and think, *I have to get back there and leave a paper before Dad finds out!*

Since they didn't get paid for their newspaper work, both boys had to earn their pocket money doing other odd jobs. Whatever they did not spend, they turned over to their father for safekeeping. Elias said he was investing the boys' money in a jelly factory in Chicago.

One day Roy demanded to see some of the profit from this investment. Elias said the factory was having some "money trouble." He could not show Roy a cent.

Now Roy understood how his brothers Herbert and Raymond had felt when Elias had not given them any of the farm land they thought they had rightfully earned. That week Roy told Walt he was running away. He told his younger brother that as soon as he got settled, he would write. He left that same night. When Flora found Roy missing the next morning, she was frantic. She wanted to call the police, but Elias would not hear of it. He told Flora she must never mention Roy's name again. As far as he was concerned he had no son called Roy at all.

Walt felt sad when Roy left, but he was developing friends and interests of his own that kept him busy. Throughout his childhood, Walt practiced drawing cartoons. Somehow, when he was fourteen, he talked his father into letting him join a Saturday morning art class at the Kansas City Art Institute. During this period, he began to spend less time at home and more time with his schoolmates.

One of his friends from school was Walt Pfeiffer. Both Walts liked to act and to put on funny skits for each other. Why not try to be performers? they asked themselves. Theaters in Kansas City had "amateur nights," when almost anybody could get up and perform on stage. There the boys hoped to try out their talents.

As often as they could, they went to movie theaters and vaudeville houses to see how the "pros" worked. Walt kept a book of notes on the comedians' jokes. After he memorized the lines and added a few of his own, he tested them out on his schoolmates.

Eventually the boys put together an act called "The Two Walts." They tried out in contests and sometimes they won!

Walt's talent for performing seemed to go hand in hand with his ability to draw. After all, they were both ways in which he could express himself artistically. If only his father could see that what he was trying to do was educational. Walt later said that Elias would go along with anything that taught you something.

But Elias refused to believe that going to theaters would advance his son's education. Before long, Walt was forbidden to attend any more theatrical performances.

That didn't stop Walt! Walt Pfeiffer later remembered how he used to help Walt sneak out of the house by climbing out of a window. "We'd be real quiet and I don't think his dad ever missed him not being in the room. When we'd get through, we'd shove him back in the window, and I'd go home."

In one of his solo acts, Walt put his drawing talent to use. He played a photographer with a fake, old-fashioned box camera. Anyone who posed in front of it got a squirt of water in his face. When he pressed the button, a bird flew out of the hole. And if someone insisted that he wanted his "picture" taken, Walt pulled a big cartoon face that he had drawn out of the camera. He would hold the cartoon up in front of the audience and say, "Looks just like him, doesn't it?"

Once, on Abraham Lincoln's birthday, Walt went to school dressed in his father's church coat and a stovepipe hat made of cardboard. In front of all the students, he imitated Lincoln and recited his most famous speech, the Gettysburg Address. Another time he used a new camera to have himself photographed as the "Little Tramp," the famous silent film character created by the actor Charlie Chaplin.

In 1917 Walt Disney was sixteen years old. He was having fun, but he was feeling restless. He wanted to be on his own. The United States had just entered into the bloody battles of World War I, alongside England and France. Roy had joined the navy and was writing letters home, but Walt never got to see them. Elias was still angry with Roy for running away from home. He burned Roy's letters as fast as they came. But on Walt's sixteenth birthday, his mother told him that she had heard that Roy was on a destroyer ship. The destroyer was escorting merchant ships across the Atlantic Ocean. Walt wished he could be out there on the Atlantic in a warship like his older brother!

About this time, Elias got "ants in his pants" again. He was getting restless in Kansas City. He had, in fact, put a good bit of money into his friend's jelly factory in Chicago. Now he was offered a job there. Once again, the family had to move.

They decided that Walt should stay on in Kansas City to finish the school term and help the man who bought Elias's newspaper delivery service break into the business. Walt would join the family after the summer when it was time to begin the new school year.

That summer Walt worked as a news butcher. News butchers were boys who sold newspapers, candy, fruit, and soft drinks to passengers on trains. For a few summers before he joined the navy, Roy had worked as a news butcher.

Walt spent the summer riding three different railroad lines across six states. From the moment he started, he enjoyed it, but everything seemed to go wrong. Any other boy would probably have gotten discouraged and given up on the first day. But not Walt. He was used to hard work.

Every day, he set up shop in the smoking car,

which was in the front of the train. Then he went from the first car to the last hawking his wares. His first day on the job was steaming hot, and Walt sold many bottles of soda. This was good for Walt, since he made money based on how many empty soda bottles he returned.

On that first day, instead of bringing the empty bottles to the first car of the train where the rest of his supplies were, he piled them in the last car to save time. When the train arrived at the end of the line, Walt was whistling a tune and feeling happy that he had sold so many bottles of soda. But when he went looking for the empties, he couldn't even find the car where he had stacked them! "Oh," the conductor said to Walt, "didn't you know that half the cars are detached at the third stop?"

Being a news butcher wasn't easy. On another day the train was full of young soldiers. Walt was able to sell them nearly all of the soda he had, but they threw their empty bottles out the window instead of giving them back to Walt!

As difficult as his work sometimes was, Walt loved this summer of travel. He never forgot the feeling of riding the rails.

When Walt joined his family in Chicago that fall, he enrolled at McKinley High School.

There he lost no time becoming an art editor of the school paper. All the time he had spent drawing as a child and the classes he had taken at the Kansas City Art Institute served him well. Now, as an art editor, he was taking one of his first steps toward becoming a serious artist.

Walt started a section in the school paper called "The Tiny Voice." It was completely filled with his patriotic cartoons, most of them urging people to support the country's involvement in World War I.

At this time, Roy was still in the navy. On one joyful occasion, Roy came in on leave and spent a lot of time with his "kid" brother. When Roy had to go back to his ship, Walt saw him off at the train station. On the platform, just as the train was pulling out, a navy officer strode up to Walt and barked at him, "Fall in, you!"

Walt couldn't believe his ears. He looked old enough to be mistaken for a sailor! From the time Flora had first told Walt that his brother Roy was in the navy aboard a destroyer, Walt had wanted to be in the navy, too. Now, even though he was under age, he tried to think of ways that he could enlist in the Great War, as it was called.

A friend, Russell Maas, came up with an idea for them both. He knew that the Red Cross

Ambulance Unit took young men who were seventeen years old.

There was just one problem: both boys were only sixteen.

Walt and Russell signed up with the Red Cross under false names. That worked out until they were asked for their parents' signatures.

Elias had two sons in the armed forces at this time. He was not about to allow Walt to become the third. "I won't sign anything. If I do, and he goes overseas, it will only be his death warrant," he said.

Flora argued with him. "If we don't sign this, Elias," she said, "we'll lose all track of him. He'll run away just like the other boys did."

"Well, you can sign if you want to, but I won't," Elias said, softening up a little bit.

And so Flora signed for herself and her husband. She wrote, "A son, Walter Elias Disney, born December 5, 1901."

When his mother wasn't looking, Walt changed the "1901" to "1900." With that little trick, he turned seventeen!

No sooner had Walt joined the Red Cross than the war ended. But ambulances were still needed in France to take care of the sick and wounded. In November of 1918, Walt sailed for Europe.

The First Movies

Walt worked for the Red Cross in France. He spent most of his time driving troops and supplies from one place to another. There was still a lot of work to do but now that the war was over, the men in the ambulance corps were in high spirits. One of the things they liked to do was play practical jokes.

On December 5, 1918, Walt celebrated his seventeenth birthday all alone—or so he thought. He was walking around the camp when a buddy came by and said, "Hey, Diz, come over to the bistro and I'll buy you a drink."

Walt did not drink much, but he went with his friend anyway. When he got to the tavern, all his friends in the corps were there singing,

"Happy Birthday to You." It was a great surprise, but there was a hidden trap.

When all the men had finished their drinking, every one of them disappeared, and Walt was left to pay the bill. He had no money and finally had to sell a pair of his shoes to pay it!

Walt was popular with his buddies. Often they called upon him for his artistic skills.

Once, just for fun, he painted a fake French medal on his leather jacket. Before he knew it, everyone wanted a painted medal, and Walt began to charge a small fee for his work. Without even planning it, Walt had set up a profitable little business for himself!

A fellow from the state of Georgia was impressed by Walt's skill and asked him for a favor. On the battlefields, he had collected a stack of helmets worn by the enemy Germans. He was selling them as souvenirs to the new troops that had arrived just as the war ended. To those recruits, a German helmet was the most prized souvenir that they could take home with them.

"Hey, Diz," the guy from Georgia said, "can you do something to these helmets so that they look real old?" Walt aged them with paint and then his buddy shot bullets through them.

Finally, Walt stuffed the bullet holes with hair he had gotten from the local barber. Now the helmets looked authentic!

The same fellow taught Walt to play poker. Walt was a quick learner. Once he won enough money in an all-night game to buy himself a tiny collie puppy. He called the puppy Carey, after one of his favorite newspaper cartoonists, Carey Orr.

Carey was so small, Walt was able to keep him in the bandage bag he carried wherever he went. The dog became so well trained, he could stand on his hind legs and raise one paw whenever anyone played the national anthem of France or the United States. He woke Walt in the morning at the moment the bugle blew. Then he fetched a clean pair of underwear and a shirt and carried them to his master between his teeth.

When Russell Maas returned to the States, he offered to take Carey with him. He would care for him, he said, until Walt decided to come home himself.

No sooner had Russell departed than Walt got homesick himself. He wrote to his mother that she would soon be seeing him again.

Walt arrived back in Chicago with armfuls of gifts. But disappointment was waiting for him: Russell informed him that his beloved dog Carey had died of distemper upon reaching the shores of America. Walt never forgot the loss of his dog.

In the meantime, Walt learned when he returned home that Elias had already figured out how Walt was to earn a living. "Son," he said, "the head of the jelly factory has a job for you. He'll pay you twenty-five dollars a week." When Walt told his father he wanted to be an artist, Elias was not happy. He had allowed Walt to study art when he was a teenager, but to earn a living as an artist was something else. Elias Disney did not see how an artist could make much money.

Walt now saw no reason to remain in Chicago. He and his father did not see eye-to-eye about his future. Roy had taken a job in a bank in Kansas City, a town that Walt knew. He decided to go there and try to get a job as an artist.

When he got to Kansas City, Walt put on his best suit of clothes and marched up to the art department of the *Kansas City Star*. This was the newspaper he had delivered on doorsteps when he was nine years old. But the paper would not even offer him an office boy's job.

Walt looked everywhere for a job. His first break came through a friend of Roy's. This man knew two commercial artists, named Louis Pessman and Bill Rubin. They were looking for an assistant.

Walt showed Rubin some of the sketches he had made of the streets of Paris when he was there with the Red Cross. He also did a few sample advertisements for them. Walt trembled with excitement when Rubin told him he could start the very next morning.

One day, on his new job, Walt sat at his drawing table practicing different ways of signing his name, wondering which would look best at the bottom of a drawing. A shy fellow with a friendly face came to peer over his shoulder. "I work here, too," he said, "and my name is Ub Iwerks" (he pronounced it "oob eye-works").

"Would you repeat that?" Walt asked.

It was a Dutch name, the strangest Walt had ever heard. He and Ub Iwerks became friends.

When the Christmas rush of that year was over, Pessman and Rubin did not have enough work for the young men to do, and they had to let both of them go. Ub Iwerks was in a panic. He had a mother to support and did not know how the two of them would survive without his paycheck.

"Listen," Walt said. "We both know a lot about drawing for advertisements now. Let's go into business ourselves."

Walt approached a newspaper called *Restaurant News*. "If you give me and my partner desks in your office," he told the editor, "we'll do all your artwork for free."

Walt's mother had put all the money he had saved while he was in France in the bank. This is exactly the moment when I need it most, Walt thought to himself. He wrote home and asked Flora to send him his savings.

She wrote back, "Your father and I want to know what you plan to do with the money."

Walt was amazed that his parents questioned him as though he were still a young boy. He was twenty years old now! He wrote back, saying that he was going into business with a partner. Then he couldn't resist adding, "After all, you know, it's *my* money."

Flora sent Walt only half of it. Still, it was enough to get the business going. Walt and Ub named their company Iwerks-Disney. When they tried the name the other way around, it sounded like an eye doctor's office!

The two men did artwork for printing companies that had no art departments. They designed advertisements and flyers.

The business went fairly well for about a month. Then Walt applied for a job as a cartoonist with the Kansas City Film Ad Company. He thought that the company might hire him *and* Ub. But the opening was for just one person. Walt got the job and Ub stayed on to run the Iwerks-Disney company. Before long, though, Iwerks-Disney went out of business. It was by a stroke of good luck that later Ub was able to join Walt at the Kansas City Film Ad Company.

The company produced one-minute animated ads that were shown in movie theaters. These ads were made by photographing paper dolls over and over again with their arms and legs in different positions. Each frame of the film showed the doll in a slightly different position. When the film was run through the camera quickly, it looked as if the figure was moving.

This was Walt's first experience with cartoon animation. He did not know then that cartoons would be the center of his career, but he did know that animation had many creative possibilities.

Walt and Ub spent a lot of time in libraries, reading everything they could find about animation. They discovered that animation had a long history. The first pictures of motion appeared on cave walls. The people who lived there in ancient times drew the same animal over and over again, in different positions, sometimes with several sets of legs. If you quickly passed your eyes over the drawings on the wall, the figures seemed to move.

Not until the 1800s were machines that successfully imitated motion invented. One invention that could do this was the zoetrope, or "live wheel." The zoetrope was a revolving cylinder with openings around the top and artwork around the bottom. As the cylinder revolved, the artwork appeared to be in motion.

Then along came Thomas Edison, one of the most famous inventors of all time. He was the inventor of the phonograph and the light bulb, and it was from his laboratory that one of the first motion picture machines came in 1889. That same year, George Eastman began to manufacture roll film, which could be used in his Kodak camera. Roll film fit on sprockets so that it could move continuously. With the invention of the motion picture machine and flexible roll film, it was now possible to make movies with live action.

In 1906 the first animated cartoon appeared. It was called *Humorous Phases of Funny Faces*. There was not much movement or story, but people found it entertaining to watch a character roll his eyes and blow smoke rings on screen. Then, in 1908, Winsor McCay made his comic strip, *Little Nemo*, into a short animated film.

By 1913, a man named Earl Hurd had invented a process that speeded up the cartoon-making process. He used two sheets of transparent celluloid, painting the background on one and the characters in motion on the other. This saved the animators a lot of time, since they no longer had to draw the background on every sheet of celluloid. Now, if the background remained the same for several scenes, the artists only had to draw the movements of the characters, and they could reuse the background they had already drawn.

While this kind of animation was being done in New York City, the Kansas City Film Ad Company was still using the old-fashioned method, moving the hands and legs on paper dolls.

Walt was becoming impatient with this early method of animation. He was interested in the new technology that Earl Hurd had invented. Walt wanted to work on celluloid ("cels" for short) and develop his own style. He borrowed an old camera from his boss and set up a lab in a garage. Then he started to make very short cartoons of funny scenes.

He took a few of these to the manager of some movie theaters in Kansas City. The man loved the funny little cartoons, which Walt called Laugh-O-Grams. These Laugh-O-Grams became so successful that Walt could afford to leave his job at the Kansas City Film Ad Company. He started his own company and named it Laugh-O-Gram after his clever creation.

To make an animated cartoon, twenty-four drawings for each second of screen time are needed. That means 14,000 drawings for a ten-minute film! No one person can do this alone. So Walt hired Ub Iwerks to work with him at Laugh-O-Gram. He also hired youngsters who wanted to learn how to draw cartoons. He told them they would not be paid until the company earned a profit.

Walt raised $25,000 from businessmen and friends. With this money, the Laugh-O-Gram Company started to animate famous fairy tales like *Little Red Riding Hood* and *Jack and the Beanstalk*. Walt also created a series of films featuring a real little girl who was surrounded by cartoon animals. He called it *Alice in Cartoonland*.

A businessman in New York City promised to pay a lot of money for six of the fairy tales. Everything looked rosy until he suddenly went out of business. He had paid Walt only a small amount of what he had promised.

This was a terrible time for Walt Disney. He now had to let all his employees go. He was forced to give up his apartment and had to sleep on a pile of pillows in the Laugh-O-Gram office. Sometimes the only food he had to eat was a bean sandwich.

Then one day a dentist phoned Walt and asked if he could make a cartoon showing children how to keep their teeth clean. "I'll pay you five hundred dollars. Come right on over and we'll settle the deal," the dentist said.

Walt was embarrassed. "I can't," he said. "I know you won't believe this, but I don't have a pair of shoes to wear. My one and only pair is at the shoemaker's downstairs."

The dentist said *he* would come to see Walt. So Walt soon found himself busy again, working on a cartoon called *Tommy Tucker's Tooth*.

This film was a success, but Walt still needed more money to pay his old debts. He tried to raise money again, but the people who had funded him before were not willing to do so again. Up until this time, Walt's brother Roy had helped him out when he needed it. Every now and then Roy sent Walt blank checks. He told Walt that he could fill them out for any amount up to thirty dollars.

Even these checks did not help now. Finally, Walt got a note from Roy saying, "It's time to call it quits, kid. You can't do any more than you've done."

Walt wrote back, "If I leave here, I'm heading for one of two places—New York or Hollywood."

One day in July 1923, Walt stepped aboard the California Limited train. He had no suit and wore pants and a checked jacket that did not match. His fake leather suitcase was nearly empty. All it had was a single shirt and a change of underwear. But Walt's head was full of ideas and plans. He was determined to get to the top in the land of fantasy—Hollywood.

The Birth of Mickey Mouse

Hollywood was the center of the movie industry. Many studios were producing movies, and it seemed there were many chances for success. Still, Walt was not sure about his future.

At first he thought he wanted to be a director, so he started knocking on the doors of famous studios. "No opening!" was the answer he got everywhere he went.

Roy was in a hospital near Los Angeles, sick with tuberculosis. He still tried to keep an eye on his twenty-two-year-old "kid" brother. He urged Walt to get back into the world of cartoons, and Walt took his advice. He had managed to hold on to one episode of *Alice in*

Cartoonland. Believing he had nothing to lose, he sent the film to Margaret J. Winkler. She was an important cartoon distributor in New York.

To his great joy, he soon received a telegram in response. Miss Winkler wrote that she was interested in the entire *Alice* series.

Walt went to the hospital and found his brother asleep on the porch. "Roy! Roy! Wake up," he said. "We're in! It's a deal!"

"What's a deal? And what do you mean when you say *we?*" Roy asked.

Walt was so excited that he couldn't stand still. "Miss Winkler will distribute six *Alices,* for starters. And I want you with me—to handle the business end. We'll call ourselves the Disney Brothers Studio. How's that?"

This was one of the most important moments in Walt's and Roy's lives. From then on, the brothers worked together with Roy as "the business end." Neither brother ever worried about a career again.

Before very long the company, now renamed Walt Disney Studio, found a home in a one-story stucco building on a quiet street outside of Los Angeles. The studio had a staff of twelve, including Ub Iwerks, whom Walt had persuaded to leave Kansas City.

The brothers were very thrifty. They shared a room and saved money by cooking for themselves. When they went out to eat, they split a main course between them.

These were tense times. One day Walt got angry about Roy's bad cooking. "That's it! I don't like this arrangement any more than you do," Roy said angrily. "And what's more, I've decided to marry my Kansas City sweetheart, Edna Francis."

There is no record of what Walt thought when he heard those words, but very soon after Roy's abrupt announcement, Walt himself was engaged to be married!

Walt met his wife-to-be at work. The studio had an opening for an "ink and paint" girl, a woman who took the animators' drawings and painted them onto the celluloid, or "cels."

"I know of someone," one of the women from the studio said. "Her name is Lillian Bounds. She is visiting from Idaho with her sister. If you hire her, you won't even have to pay her carfare, because she is staying just a few streets away."

And so Lilly came to work for the Disneys. She earned fifteen dollars a week. She was slim, with short dark hair and a lively manner. One day, when she and Walt were the only two people in the studio, Walt took her by surprise. He stooped down and kissed her on the cheek. She blushed a bright red.

That evening, Walt drove Lilly home. As he pulled up in front of her house, he said, "You know, I would come in and meet your family, but I don't have a suit."

"What you're wearing is just fine," Lilly said, but Walt did not agree. That night, he left Lilly at her door.

A short while later Walt bought himself a forty-dollar suit. He was so proud of it that when he finally did meet Lilly's sister and her family, all he could think to say was, "How do you like my suit?"

One night, driving back from a movie date, Lilly commented that Walt's old Ford was pretty shabby.

"Which would you rather have me buy," Walt asked, "a new car or an engagement ring for you?"

Lilly had no trouble making up her mind. "A ring!" she said quickly. They were married soon after that.

The studio had made more than four dozen *Alice* films when Miss Winkler and her new husband and partner, Charles Mintz, came up with a suggestion. How about an all-cartoon series, with a rabbit as the hero?

Walt thought that was a fine idea and set to work with Ub Iwerks on a cartoon character with so much personality, he seemed to be almost human. He was plump, furry, and lovable. His name was Oswald, the Lucky Rabbit.

Often, Walt would work far into the night on his new character. Lilly would drive by to pick up her husband and fall asleep waiting for him. When Walt woke her, she'd ask sleepily, "What time is it?" "Oh, not very late," Walt would lie, "maybe ten o'clock." Then the couple would drive home just before the dawn broke.

Oswald the Rabbit bcame popular all over the country. But Charles Mintz had a nasty plot that Walt knew nothing about. Mintz had secretly arranged to lure away all the Disney artists by offering them more money than Walt was paying them. He planned to do this if Walt would not accept his business conditions.

When Walt went to New York to settle on a price for some new *Oswald* films, Mintz surprised him by offering a sum that was less than what he was already receiving.

"I don't get it," Walt said, puzzled. "The pictures are earning lots of money." Then Mintz sprang his trap. "Either you come with me at my price," Mintz threatened, "or I'll take your company away from you." Walt took these words seriously. Charles Mintz could steal his staff *and* his Oswald because Walt had only *drawn* the rabbit for him. Charles Mintz had all the rights to the Oswald character, which meant that he, not Walt, owned Oswald. There was no way Walt could produce another film without Oswald.

Walt felt beaten. He trudged back to the New York hotel where he and Lilly were staying and told her the story. He threw his hat down on the bed in anger. "I'll never work for someone else again," he vowed.

"So, what will you do?" Lilly asked.

"Get the first train out of here, is what we're going to do. If I have to hire new artists and start a new series, I can't lose any time."

He sent a telegram to Roy: "Everything's okay. Coming home."

Lilly was confused by Walt's words. "That's a funny thing to say: 'Everything's okay,' " Lilly commented. To her, things had never looked worse.

Walt put his arm around her. "Just wait," he said mysteriously.

The story goes that Mickey Mouse, the world's most famous cartoon character, was born on that train ride back to Hollywood.

The Three Little Pigs Wins an Oscar

Walt later recalled how the merry little figure of a mouse came to life in his mind as the train took him and his wife west to California. "The wheels turned to the tune of it. 'Chug, chug, *mouse*, chug, chug, *mouse*.' The whistle screeched, 'A *m-m-mowa-ouse*.' By the time the train had reached the Middle West, I had dressed my dream mouse in a pair of velvet pants and two huge pearl buttons."

Walt thought that Mortimer Mouse was a fine name for his creation. But Lilly said, "Mortimer sounds wrong. It's . . . it's not catchy." They tossed names back and forth for a while until Walt said, "Well then—how about Mickey? Mickey Mouse."

It was Ub Iwerks who created the early Mickey Mouse drawings. Since the figure would have to be drawn about fourteen thousand times for each short film, the design had to be simple. The basis of Mickey's shape was two large circles and two small ones. The two large ones were for the body and head, the small ones for the big black ears. Mickey was given a long thin tail, arms and legs like rubbery hoses, and a puffy hand with four fingers, instead of five. (In later cartoons, he wore white gloves.) With Mickey's large face and eyes, he had all the appeal of an adorable child.

The Disney studio was in the middle of making the first Mickey Mouse films when a very special event took place. This event changed the entire history of movie-making.

Up until this time, films had all been silent. When an actor spoke, his words were written on the screen but not heard by the audience. In some theaters, someone played the piano or organ as the soundless movie rolled along.

Then on October 6, 1927, Al Jolson, a popular singing star, appeared in a movie called *The Jazz Singer*. When Jolson talked and sang, audiences actually heard his voice! Sound film had been invented. It was an important new chapter in the history of the movies.

Walt heard about the new "talking film" while he was making *Steamboat Willie,* a silent film, starring Mickey Mouse. He stopped right in the middle of everything. He knew what he wanted to do now: make *Steamboat Willie* with sound! But more than that, Walt wanted to *synchronize* the sound, so that the music and voices would match the action in the film. Walt was not the first animator to make a cartoon with sound. Someone had already done that, but the music was not synchronized; it didn't match the action. Walt knew he could do better, and with the help of his staff he worked out a way. Now he needed to try it out.

One summer evening Walt and some of the men he worked with called their wives together and asked them to be their audience. First they hung a sheet in the garage doorway to act as a movie screen. Then they began the movie. While the guests sat on the lawn and watched, the men stood behind the screen and played music to go along with the movie. They hit cowbells, blew whistles, and scrubbed away at washboards. The music they played matched exactly what the characters on the screen were doing, and it ended at exactly the moment that the film ended. The sound was synchronized perfectly! Walt's experiment had worked!

On September 29, 1928, *Steamboat Willie* opened at the Colony Theater in New York. It was one of the earliest sound films, and it was a tremendous success. Film producers loved the Mickey Mouse character. They wanted to hire Walt to make the cartoons for them.

But Walt had learned his lesson when he lost Oswald the Rabbit to Mr. Mintz. He refused every offer. "I'm going to own my own films from now on," he said.

Now the Disney studio was doing well, but the rest of the country was not. The United States was going through a terrible time called the Great Depression. Twelve million people were out of work. Many of these people were homeless and hungry.

While life for most people was very difficult, life in the movie business was not. More than ever, people wanted to escape their troubles by going to the movies.

The Mickey Mouse cartoons had become a popular success for Disney, and they helped lift the spirit of the nation. But Walt didn't want to do just one character and one kind of animated cartoon. In 1929, he started his staff on a new series of musical cartoons, called *Silly Symphonies*, in which he experimented with different characters, stories, and techniques.

In 1932, Walt tried out the new full-color film process, Technicolor, in the cartoon *Flowers and Trees*. It was so popular it became the first cartoon ever to win the Academy Award.

In 1933, Walt Disney produced what would be the most famous short cartoon of all time, *The Three Little Pigs*. This new cartoon had both sound *and* color. The film's song, "Who's Afraid of the Big Bad Wolf?" became the number one popular hit song in the country. To most people, the big bad wolf was like the Great Depression: If the three little pigs could keep the wolf from blowing their house down, then maybe ordinary Americans could keep poverty and hunger from their doors.

The Three Little Pigs won an Oscar for best cartoon of the year. That same year, a few days after Walt's thirty-second birthday, Lilly had their first child, a baby girl named Diane Marie.

In the hospital, Lilly began to say, "I feel I ought to have given you . . ."

Walt thought she was going to say, ". . . ought

to have given you a boy," and he began to protest. But Lilly was thinking of *The Three Little Pigs* and finished her sentence, ". . . ought to have given you triplets!"

Three years later the Disneys adopted a baby girl, Sharon. With two children, the family was complete.

Walt Disney looks through one of his first movie cameras. (1925)

Walt Disney and an assistant cameraman from Walt's "Laugh-O-Gram" film company.

The Multiplane camera that was invented to make animated films appear more true to life.

"Ink and Paint" women paint drawings on celluloid, "cels."

Walt Disney and the "voices" of *The Three Little Pigs*. From left to right: Dorothy Compton, second pig; Pinto Colvic, third pig and the "Big Bad Wolf"; and Mary Moder, the first pig. Frank Churchill, who wrote and played the score, is at right.

Walt sketches Bambi and Faline for his 1942 movie, *Bambi*.

Walt Disney and his family arrive in Paris. From left to right: Walt, Lillian, and daughters Sharon and Diane.

Portrait of Walt Disney.

Walt Disney plays with models of the stars of his first animated films.

Men at work on the model for Euro-Disneyland. The park opened outside of Paris, France, in 1992.

Walt Disney's world-famous cartoon characters mourn the death of their creator in a cartoon by artist Don Wright that appeared in *The Miami News* on December 16, 1966.

"Disney's Folly"

During the Depression, people had very little money and movie theaters were having trouble getting the crowds they needed to make money. So the owners of the theaters started the "double feature." This meant that two pictures could be seen for the price of one. After they had rented two movies, however, the theaters discovered that there was not much money left to rent the short cartoons that they played along with them.

Walt was worried. Not only were cartoons not in demand as much as before, but they were also getting more and more expensive to make. What should the Disney studio do? As usual, Walt came up with a solution. This was the perfect time, he figured, to do a full-length animated film.

When Walt was a newsboy in Kansas City, he was invited along with other newsboys to see the silent film of the fairy tale *Snow White*. He had fallen in love with the story, and to him it seemed perfect for animation. It had everything: tragedy, romance, and humor.

One evening he gathered his artists around and told them about his version of *Snow White and the Seven Dwarfs*. He acted out all the parts himself, and by the time he was finished, everyone's eyes were damp with tears.

The great success of *The Three Little Pigs* and all the Mickey Mouse cartoons had led to the studio's rapid growth. When *Snow White* went into production there were 750 people working for Walt Disney!

As this famous movie took shape there were many meetings, many notes taken, and many sketches drawn. Little puppet models were made of the seven dwarfs to develop their personalities. Well-known European artists were called in to paint backgrounds.

To get the clear and childlike voice he wanted for the heroine, Walt listened to many hopeful singers from a speaker he installed in his office.

He finally chose Adriana Caselotti, an eighteen-year-old girl who was trained to sing opera. Popular comedians provided the voices for the seven dwarfs.

A special camera called a multiplane was invented to make *Snow White* look three dimensional and more true-to-life than the short cartoons. It was a huge contraption that took up an entire room. To show someone approaching a distant castle, the castle would be painted on a bottom plane, a layer of cellophane. Then the camera would zoom in on the castle, passing through several different planes of cellophane, each painted with different scenery. As the camera passed through the changing planes, the viewer seemed to move toward the castle, with the changing scenery passing by.

Walt tried out this new camera for one of his cartoons called *The Old Mill*. The short was so good, it won an Academy Award on its own.

At first Walt thought *Snow White* would cost about half a million dollars. That was a lot of money to raise, and Roy protested. Later, when it looked as if that amount would not be nearly enough, Roy had a talk with Walt. He said people were starting to laugh at them because they were spending so much money. They were making fun of the *Snow White* project and had named it Disney's Folly.

"Let them call it 'Disney's Folly' or anything else they want to," one of Walt's friends advised him. "It keeps everybody wondering what kind of picture this is. If they keep wondering, they'll keep talking and before you know it you'll have a million dollars worth of free publicity."

When Roy saw that Walt was going ahead no matter what, he set up a meeting between Walt and Joe Rosenberg, a vice-president of the Bank of America. Mr. Rosenberg wanted to see the movie first. If he liked it, the bank would lend the studio the money it needed to finish it.

"I just can't show it," Walt said. "All we've got is bits and pieces. That's worse than nothing."

"Well, you're going to have to do it," Roy insisted. "There's no other way."

Mr. Rosenberg came to the studio's projection room and was shown an unfinished version of *Snow White*. The banker watched, while Walt acted out all the different parts and sang songs to fill in the gaps. Finally it was over and the two men walked in silence side by side to the parking lot.

Mr. Rosenberg got into his car and started the motor. He hadn't yet talked about the loan. Walt's heart was sinking by the minute.

Finally he said, "You know, Walt, that picture of yours is going to make us a potful of money!"

Walt sighed in relief.

Snow White and the Seven Dwarfs opened on December 7, 1937, and played to packed audiences at Radio City Music Hall in New York. After showing there for five weeks, it ran in Paris, France, for thirty-one weeks.

Audiences all around the world loved the seven dwarfs and their entertaining antics. They were charmed by songs like "Heigh Ho, Heigh Ho, It's Off to Work We Go." And they were thrilled when the wicked queen met her just end and Snow White was recalled to life by the handsome prince.

Four years in the making, the picture was just about perfect. It earned eight million dollars in ticket sales. This was a remarkable amount of money since movie tickets were just twenty-five cents for adults and ten cents for children in those days.

Walt received another Academy Award for this latest masterpiece. This time there were eight Oscars—one for Snow White and seven little Oscars mounted on steps for the dwarfs.

The award was presented to him by Shirley Temple, a popular ten-year-old actress. With her prim white collar and mop of curls, Shirley Temple was more at ease on the awards stage than the famous film maker. "Please don't be so nervous, Mr. Disney," she whispered in his ear as she put the trophies in his trembling hands.

After *Snow White*, the Disney Studio continued to make animated movies. But at the same time, they were developing new characters for their cartoon shorts. There was the bright bloodhound, Pluto the Pup, and a sweet but not-so-clever dog, Goofy. The most famous of the characters was Donald Duck. While Mickey Mouse's voice was done by Walt himself, Donald's distinctive voice was provided by Clarence Nash, a man who had imitated animal sounds on the radio.

Donald was a contrast to the super-nice Mickey. He was a show-off; he was stingy; and he had a bad temper. Audiences loved Donald right from the start, and nearly one hundred short films were made with this web-footed hero.

The next two full-length movies, *Pinocchio*

and *Fantasia,* cost a lot of money to make but did not bring in large profits. *Dumbo* and *Bambi* did better. Today these movies are considered classics. Children and adults of all ages love them.

In 1939 the Disney studio was sixteen years old. It had over one thousand employees and was still growing. It had a big, new home in Burbank, California. It looked more like a miniature city than a movie studio! Everything was specialized: There was one building for animation, another for inking and painting, still another for cutting and editing, and so on. It had a modern air-conditioning system and its own sewage disposal plant, and electrical works.

Elias Disney, now nearly eighty, could not believe his sons were so successful. After looking at all the hammering and sawing and brick-laying for the new studio, he asked Walt, "How on earth are you going to support this big place with those cartoons of yours? Aren't you afraid you'll go broke?"

"Well, if I do go broke," Walt said, teasing his father, "—just look at all these rooms along the long corridors. If I have to, I can always sell the place to be used as a hospital!"

By the end of 1939 a second world war had

begun. It brought even more disaster to the world than the first war when Walt had worked as an ambulance driver. Disney films were about to be shown in major European cities, but the bookings were canceled. It seemed as though Elias's fears had come true: the studio was in financial trouble.

There was another kind of trouble brewing as well. Disney artists, among the finest in their field, loved their jobs. But they were not happy with their low pay. And they were not always happy with their boss, Walt Disney.

Walt was becoming more and more like the father he had so feared in his childhood. He was distant and critical and wanted to run everything himself. Walt was a loner, and he was not easy to talk to. The workers wanted a union to represent them, but Walt had little use for unions.

On May 29, 1941, the artists in the studio went on strike. The strike lasted nine bitter weeks. Finally, the artists won the right to have a union.

While the studio was on strike, the Second World War was getting more serious.

In December, Pearl Harbor, part of the U.S. territory of Hawaii, was bombed by the Japanese, and the United States formally declared itself to be at war.

One day, shortly after war was declared, the Disney household received a call from the studio manager. "Walt," the manager said, "the army wants to move into our place. I said I had to call you before they could do that. And *they* said sorry, they'd move into the studio whether you liked it or not."

Walt had not *sold* the studio, as he had joked with his father that he might. Nevertheless, that week seven hundred soldiers, part of an anti-aircraft unit stationed in the Los Angeles area, took over part of the Burbank studios along with fourteen trucks and an immense amount of equipment.

Donald Duck Joins Up

The soldiers stayed for seven months. On the day they left, Walt rushed over to his office to take a call from a high official in the navy. "We'd like to hire you to make some films for us on how to spot enemy aircraft," the man said. "We need the first ones in three months, so you can start right now."

"I'd be glad to start," Walt replied. "But I don't have the first idea about what to do, sir."

"I'll send an expert over immediately, and he'll tell you everything there is to know about our anti-aircraft system."

The aircraft films were no sooner finished when another call came, this one from the office of the Secretary of the Treasury. "We want to sell people on the idea of paying their taxes, and also paying on time. Can you work up a cartoon on that?"

For this film, Disney decided to use one of his top cartoon stars, Donald Duck. America had fallen in love with Donald's raspy voice and quick temper. He had appeared in several dozen film shorts. If this difficult duck could be convinced to file his income tax return promptly, Walt thought that average Americans would also be convinced and follow his example. They did.

Donald Duck also appeared in a war film called *Der Fuehrer's Face*, which made fun of the German leader, Adolf Hitler. In it Donald dreams he is living in Germany and forced to work for the cruel Nazis. He sees the swastika, the Nazi symbol everywhere: on the wallpaper, on fireplugs, on picket fences. Then he wakes up in his red-white-and-blue pajamas and realizes it was all a nightmare.

Walt put his other famous cartoon characters to work in shorts, too. The Disney studio turned out dozens of instruction films with patriotic messages for nurses, pilots, navigators, and others in the armed forces.

* * *

By the end of the war, Walt was exhausted. He needed a rest badly. Taking his daughter Sharon along, he took a trip north to Alaska.

In Alaska, Walt met Al and Elma Milotte, husband-and-wife photographers who also ran a camera shop.

"How would you like to make some pictures for me up here?" Walt asked.

"What kind of pictures?" Al Milotte asked.

"Oh, anything about Alaska—mining, fishing, building roads. . . ."

Walt returned to his studio in Burbank and the Milottes began to shoot miles of film footage and send it down to him.

After viewing the first reels, Walt wired the photographers: "You've got too many mines, too many roads. Give me more animals."

After Mr. Milotte read Walt's telegram, he remembered the fur seals of the Pribilof Islands. Each year they came to the Islands to mate, to fight, and to give birth to their babies. Then they seemed to disappear. It was a mystery.

Walt had a hunch that the public would find the seals fascinating. He wired to Alaska: "More seals!" Finally the studio put together the best footage into a thirty-minute film called *Seal Island.*

Roy went to New York to try to interest theaters in the film. He phoned Walt, sounding dismal. "No one wants the picture, Walt. They all say, 'Who wants to look at seals playing house on a bare rock?' I'm about ready to give up."

But Walt was confident that, once again, he had something the public would like. "Hey, Roy, pal, come back to sunny California," he said. "Maybe it'll improve your mood."

Walt found a theater in California, which agreed to show *Seal Island,* and the movie ended up winning yet another Academy Award for the studio. The morning after the award ceremony, Walt strode into Roy's office and tossed his Oscar at him like a football. "Still scared the movie won't make it?" he teased.

Other "True Life Adventures" followed. These were the first commercial nature films ever made. And once Walt began, the public wanted more and more. There was *The Living Desert, The Vanishing Prairie,* and *Secrets of Life,* among others.

The Milottes, now working with a team of Disney photographers, traveled all over the world for Walt. They would go where the animals lived and would wait for hours, even weeks to get the right kind of shots.

Once, while making a short called *Beaver Valley,* Al Milotte got impatient with one of the animals. The beaver was busy as could be, but the moment Al Milotte's camera was ready to roll, the beaver would stop gnawing at the tree and go off to play. Milotte was getting tired of waiting. He pulled at the twigs of the tree and set up a whooshing noise. Then he yelled, *"Do it again,* you pest! Hit that tree, hear me?" The beaver began to gnaw at the tree again, and Milotte got his shot.

After the Second World War, Walt Disney began to work more with live-action films. In 1946 he made *Song of the South,* and in 1949 he made a film called *So Dear to My Heart.* Both of the films combined live action with animation. Then, in 1950, Walt decided to make *Treasure Island,* a film that was completely live-action, with no animation at all.

Walt hired the best British actors he could find, and *Treasure Island* was a big success. The Disney studios earned a lot of praise and money from this handsome movie. Not only was this

his first all live-action film, *Treasure Island* was Walt's first adventure film.

In the next three years Walt produced three other live-action films for children, *The Story of Robin Hood, The Sword and the Rose*, and *Rob Roy. Time* magazine wrote, "they were amazingly good. Each was just what a children's classic is supposed to be, a breath of healthy air blown in from the meadows of far away and long ago."

Maybe Walt was able to make films that children loved so much because there was still a bit of the child in him. In December, 1947, he wrote in his Christmas letter to his sister Ruth: "I bought myself a birthday-Christmas present—something I've wanted all my life—an electric train. I have set it up in one of the outer rooms adjoining my office. It's a freight train with a whistle, and real smoke comes out of the smokestack. It's just wonderful!"

Ever since he had been a "news butcher" as a boy in Kansas City, Walt had loved everything about trains. But soon after he bought himself the toy train he described to Ruth, he decided that was not enough: he wanted the real thing.

Lilly was not very enthusiastic at the thought of a train tearing up her lawns and plowing through her flower beds. The family was about to move into a larger house. They had bought property large enough for the train, but it was hard to convince Lilly that a locomotive belonged in their backyard.

Walt was determined to have his way. One day Lilly and the girls were surprised when Walt turned up at the dinner table with a written contract, ready for them to sign. No contract, no new house, he said. Lilly, Diane, and Sharon looked wide-eyed at the long document with its big, legal-sounding words. "Wait, I'll get a pen," Lilly said. Then Walt folded up the contract and put it in his pocket. He said they didn't actually have to sign the contract after all. He knew he had won his case!

Walt helped to build much of the train, which was modeled on a nineteenth-century design. Each car was authentic in every detail, although somewhat smaller than the real thing. He even had little newspapers of the period printed up and put on racks. He named the engine the Lilly Belle, hoping to please his wife.

But Walt was not about to stop there. Building a train in his backyard inspired him to do some building on a much larger scale.

The Magic Kingdom

On Sunday mornings, Walt often took his daughters, Diane and Sharon, to amusement parks. While his daughters whirled around on the rides, Walt strolled through the grounds. He noticed that everyone but the young children looked bored. The parks were dirty with litter and sometimes smelled bad. Why should an amusement park be shabby and depressing? he asked himself. Walt wanted to build an amusement park of his own.

Whenever he took trips to different parts of the world, he visited zoos, circuses, and fairs. Soon, a plan for his own park began to take shape in his mind.

At first Walt planned to build the park on the

studio's grounds, and he thought he would call it Mickey Mouse Park. But by the time Walt finished thinking it through, it was clear to everyone that this park would be so big that it would not fit in the space near the studio. Walt decided to look for space someplace else. He finally decided to call the new enterprise Disneyland.

"The park means a lot to me," he told a reporter. "When you wrap up a picture you're through. But a park is never finished. It's alive and can grow. It will get better and more beautiful as I find out what the public likes."

By the summer of 1953 Walt had a planning group working on a theme park idea, but he still did not know where he would get the money to build the park. At the end of one sleepless night, he telephoned Roy. "I've found the answer to our problems," he said. "You have?" Roy asked doubtfully.

"Yes, it's television. Television is going to help us finance the park."

In those days TV was still new, and most moviemakers thought it was not good for their business. They feared that people would stay home and watch TV, instead of going to the movies.

Walt thought differently about television. He saw great opportunities in it for the studio and for the park. He decided to ask the television networks to help finance the park. In exchange, he would provide them with his own TV programs.

The American Broadcasting Company (ABC) was interested in Walt's plan. One day he received a call from an executive vice president. "I hear you need money to build your park. Give us Mickey Mouse plus the Disney name and see how great we both do."

ABC gave the Disney studio a seven-year contract. The television show, like the park, would be called "Disneyland" and would be a perfect way to spread the word to the public about the park. For years, Walt had been the voice of Mickey Mouse, behind the scenes. Now he could speak in his own voice, in front of the cameras, as master of ceremonies of the new show "Disneyland."

Walt's scouts traveled all across the state of California to find the perfect spot for the Disneyland park. They finally located one hundred acres of land in Orange County, just outside of Los Angeles. Walt hired a team of architects and planners and traveled with them around the country studying other amusement parks. He called his crew "Imagineers."

At home he talked of nothing but the park. Walt said he wanted the park to be "something of a fair, an exhibition, a playground, a community center, and a museum of living facts." But it was hard to take him seriously when he mentioned fairy castles and real steamboats going down real rivers with mechanical hippos popping out of them. It wasn't until she saw workmen actually moving mountains on the Disneyland site that Diane Disney realized her father could make almost anything come true if he tried hard enough.

Disneyland opened at Anaheim, California, on July 18, 1955, with the paint and concrete barely dry.

There were 30,000 visitors the first day. Thousands of others watched the opening on ABC television. Within six months, one million people had passed through its gates!

Kings and queens, princes and princesses came, as well as many heads of state. People from all over the world flocked to the gates of the Magic Kingdom. Thirty years after the opening, the average number of guests at Disneyland was 23 million a year—more people than visited the whole country of England during the same time!

The theme park was like a world built from scratch. The mountains, lakes, and rivers were designed by architects and built with the help of bulldozers and steam shovels. Most of the animals seen from the rides were not real, but they were so cleverly made that they seemed to breathe like real animals.

It was a world that mirrored Walt's own life: the Midwest town where he had spent his happiest years, the romance of the railroads he had traveled, the fairy tales he brought to life in his cartoons.

Disneyland looked like a fantastic movie set. The old-fashioned small-town Main Street at the center of Disneyland had horse-drawn streetcars and steam engines puffing along. From a central "town square" visitors saw the Magic Kingdom's four "lands": Fantasyland, Frontierland, Adventureland, and Tomorrowland.

At Adventureland, Walt tried out a new invention called audio-animatronics. This new technology used magnetic tape (similar to the kind used in tape recorders) to make lifelike objects move and talk.

The most remarkable example of audio-animatronics was a show called "Moments with Mr. Lincoln."

Here a life-sized figure of Abraham Lincoln moved its arms and legs and parts of its face. It got up and spoke to the audience with realistic gestures, as if the sixteenth president had come to life after one hundred years!

One day the Lincoln figure did seem to take on a life of his own. He went haywire due to a mechanical problem. He smashed chairs and struck out wildly at some of the workers in the area. Fortunately this did not happen in front of an audience!

The Kingdom of Disney

Disneyland was one of the biggest and most successful projects Walt Disney ever attempted. Now that it was open and receiving great praise, Walt moved on to yet another project.

In October, 1955, he introduced a new children's television program. It was called "The Mickey Mouse Club." He needed twenty-four talented children, called Mouseketeers, for the show. But he did not want the usual child actors who flooded the movie studios of Hollywood.

He told his producer, "Look around the schools for kids with good personalities. Watch them at recess. The one who's the center of attention, who is leading all the action, that's the one we want."

"The Mickey Mouse Club" was a hit. At five o'clock weekdays most of America's television sets were tuned in to it. Listeners memorized the chant that began the show: M-I-C, K-E-Y, M-O-U-S-E. Mouse-ear caps sold at the rate of 24,000 a day. The most popular Mouseketeer, Annette Funicello, received as many as six thousand letters a month from her fans!

Walt had been a hit in the world of movies. Now he was a master of television and creator of one of the largest amusement parks in the world as well. He was a wealthy man, but he still remembered the early days when he barely had enough money to keep going. Once, when he was driving home from the studio, he saw a fancy car in a showroom window. "Gee, I wish I could afford that," he said to himself. He drove a few blocks before he suddenly realized he *could* afford the car. He went back and bought it!

Through the television years, Walt continued to make movies, too. In the 1940s when Diane Disney was a little girl, Walt had found her reading a book and giggling out loud. The book was *Mary Poppins,* written by an Australian writer, P. L. Travers, about a nanny who could fly. As soon as Walt read the book, he knew he had to make a movie out of it. It took Walt twenty years to convince Mrs. Travers to let him make the movie. It finally appeared in 1964.

Walt used the best talent he could find. He was very lucky to get Julie Andrews, the young English actress and singer, to play the "practically perfect" governess. She had been successful on the stage in *My Fair Lady* and *Camelot*, but this would be her first movie.

The writer of the screenplay modeled the father in the story after Walt himself. Mr. Banks was stubborn and crusty, but he had his sweet side, too. And, like Walt in his earlier years, he was "always in trouble with the bank."

Mary Poppins was a delightful nanny. She could fly and make magical things happen. This gave the Disney studio a chance to pull out its whole bag of special effects tricks.

The movie received thirteen Academy Award nominations in 1964. Julie Andrews won the award for best actress, and *Mary Poppins* became one of the most popular films of all time.

But even with this great success, Walt was

restless and looking toward new horizons. In 1965, a Florida journalist "broke" a story in the *Orlando Sentinel* newspaper. She revealed that Walt Disney had bought acres and acres of land in the area and was planning to build a theme park many times the size of Disneyland.

Walt was unhappy that all around the California park flashy hotels and cheap forms of entertainment had sprung up. He wanted an unspoiled place where whole families could stay for days and even weeks. He had promised himself that if he built another park, he was "going to buy up a whole state, not just a few orange groves."

Elias and Flora Disney had gotten married near the Florida town of Kissimmee. Perhaps that is why Walt chose Florida for the future site of Walt Disney World. First he bought up 30,000 acres of land. Next he got the permission of the local government to run the area like a small city. Then the bulldozers went to work to change Osceola County from a wilderness into the largest theme park in the world.

Walt had an equally grand dream for the land next to the park. He wanted to build a city of the future, with the name EPCOT, which stood for Experimental Prototype Community of Tomorrow. It would be, he said, "a showcase for American industry and research." Every improvement and invention at EPCOT would be twenty-five years ahead of its time.

Walt's life was completely given over to these projects. Wherever he went, he would jot down notes on pieces of paper or napkins and stuff them into his pockets to be talked about later. He had a locked room behind his office especially set aside for his EPCOT work. The walls of the room were covered with maps, drawings, and photographs, all covered with Walt's notes. He even talked about EPCOT in his sleep!

Perhaps Walt worked so hard on EPCOT because he was growing old and was afraid that he would not live to see it completed. He was in his mid-sixties, and people at the studio thought that Walt was aging. He now suffered from neck pain and leg troubles. When he went to consult a doctor about these complaints, the doctor took complete X-rays of his body. The X-rays showed that Walt had a damaged lung.

Walt had been known for his cough. In fact, the workers in his studio could always tell when he was coming along the corridor by the *kaf-kaf* sound of his cough. Now Walt had lung cancer, and he needed an operation.

The operation was not successful. But Walt kept working until the moment of his death.

His last conversation was with Roy—about EPCOT. "You must see it through for me," he said.

Roy nodded. "But you'll be up and around before you know, Walt," he told his brother. Sadly, Roy did not believe his own words. He wondered how the Disney empire would get along without the man who had built it.

Walt's frail body gave out in the early morning hours of December 15, 1966, just ten days after his sixty-fifth birthday. He left a shocked and grieving world behind.

After his death, a Paris newspaper ran a picture of Mickey Mouse crying and wrote, "All the children in the world are mourning. And we have never felt so close to them." An editorial in Italy called Walt "a poet-magician who brought the world of fable alive." The *New York Times* said he was "a legend in his own lifetime."

Walt Disney World opened on October 23, 1971. Beneath the spires of Cinderella's Castle, a world symphony orchestra, with its members taken from many countries, played Disney tunes. Roy, now seventy-eight, spoke of his brother as a genius who "was never pushed off his course." Walt always plowed ahead with his visions and saw them through.

Walt Disney World followed many of Walt's plans in detail. No automobiles or buses were permitted, since Walt didn't want any problems with air pollution. Instead, a sleek monorail train shuttled people between the Magic Kingdom and their hotels.

Efficient People Mover cars moved quietly across the grounds. Based on a German model, the People Mover was later used at the Intercontinental Airport in Houston, Texas.

The Florida park was like a small city. It was, in fact, twice the size of New York City's Manhattan Island. Underneath this city was a huge basement with repair shops, cables, and pipes. There was a modern waste-disposal system with aerojet tubes that whisked garbage away to a central compacting unit.

EPCOT Center, covering 260 acres all by itself, was not exactly the community that Walt had imagined. But many of his ideas for EPCOT were now part of Disneyland and Walt Disney World. Opening in October 1982, EP-

COT was divided into two parts. The first part, Future World, was the "showcase for American industry" that Walt had hoped for. Seven corporations presented exhibits designed to show the latest in science and technology. In the second part, the World Showcase, eleven countries displayed their crafts, architecture, and other ways of life to the thousands of EPCOT visitors that crowded in each day.

In the 1980s the Disney studio enjoyed great success in Hollywood. A new Disney cable television channel boasted four million viewers. Walt would have been delighted to see Disneyland open in Tokyo, Japan, in 1983. And he would have been excited about the plans for a Euro-Disneyland just outside of Paris, France. In 1988, Walt Disney World created Birthdayland in honor of Mickey Mouse's sixtieth birthday. There is a party there every day of the year. In the new Memory Room visitors can find samples of old Mickey Mouse films and souvenirs of the lively little mouse's career. On May 1, 1989, the Disney MGM Studios Theme Park opened at Walt Disney World. There, guests can see for themselves just how movies are made. They can visit the special effects, sound effects, and animation theaters to see artists, animators, and technicians at work. Or they can take the Great Movie Ride through some of the world's best loved films. Walt Disney's work has come a long way from the cluttered Laugh-O-Gram office in Kansas City!

What was it that made Walt Disney different from other cartoonists or other business people? Perhaps it was that Walt Disney was like a great magician. His work was like a mirror that gave all people, young and old alike, the chance to see the fantasy and enchantment in their lives.

And his magic lives on.

Highlights in the Life of
WALT DISNEY

1901   Walter Elias Disney is born on December 5.

1918   Walt goes to France to work for the Red Cross Ambulance Corps.

1919   Walt gets his first job as an artist, and later starts the Laugh-O-Gram company.

1923   Walt creates the *Alice in Cartoonland* series.

He moves to Hollywood and forms the Walt Disney Studio.

1925   Walt marries Lilly Bounds.

1927   Walt creates the *Oswald the Lucky Rabbit* series.

1928   Mickey Mouse is born.

Steamboat Willie opens in New York City.

1933   Walt creates *The Three Little Pigs.*

A daughter, Diane Marie Disney, is born.

1934   Donald Duck makes his debut.

1936   A second daughter, Sharon Disney, is adopted.

1937   Walt creates *Snow White and the Seven Dwarfs.*

1940   Walt creates *Pinocchio.*

The Disney Studio moves to Burbank.

1941 Walt creates *Dumbo*.

1942 Walt creates *Bambi*.

1948 Walt produces his first nature film, *Seal Island*.

1954 The "Disneyland" television show is aired.

1955 Disneyland opens in Anaheim, California.
"The Mickey Mouse Club" TV show begins.

1964 Walt produces *Mary Poppins*.

1966 Walt Disney dies on December 15.

1971 Walt Disney World opens in Orlando, Florida.

1982 EPCOT Center opens in Orlando, Florida.

1983 Tokyo Disneyland opens in Japan.

1986 Walt Disney Productions changes its name to Walt Disney Company.

1989 The Disney MGM Studios Theme Park opens at Walt Disney World in Florida.

1992 Euro-Disneyland opens near Paris, France.

1996 Walt Disney Company purchases Capital Cities/ABC, making Disney the biggest media company in the United States.

New and older Disney movies and television programs continue to delight people of all ages year after year.

For Further Study

More Books to Read

The Man Behind the Magic: The Story of Walt Disney.
  Katherine Barrett and Richard Greene (Viking)

The Super Showmen. Bennett Wayne (Garrard)

Walt Disney. Jim Fanning (Chelsea House)

Walt Disney. Maxine P. Fisher (Franklin Watts)

Walt Disney. Greta Walker (Putnam)

Walt Disney: An American Original. Bob Thomas
  (Hyperion)

Walt Disney: A Biography. Barbara Ford (Walker)

Walt Disney: Master of Make-Believe.
  Elizabeth Montgomery (Garrard)

Walt Disney World and Epcot Center. Valerie Childs
  (Random House Value)

Videos

Disney's Storybook Classics. (Walt Disney Home Video)

Snow White and the Seven Dwarfs.
  (Walt Disney Home Video)

Index

98

99